HAPPY QUOTES

By Kristen Griffin

Illustrated by Giorgia Isacchi

For information on reprints, bulk orders, or school and organization purchases, please contact: hello@happyhappyeverything.com

ISBN 979-8-9959720-0-6
Written by Kristen Griffin
Illustrated by Giorgia Isacchi

First Edition

Happy Happy Everything Inc.
Naples, FL, USA
happyhappyeverything.com

To Gregory and Lily,
this book was made for you
with so much love!

May you always have a
happy quote to make you
smile.

MAY
ALL YOUR
HAPPY WISHES
IN YOUR HEART
COME TRUE!

YOU CAN DO
THIS, YOU
GOT THIS,
THE POWER'S
INSIDE OF
YOU!

YOU ARE
SO SO SO
SPECIAL!

DREAM REALLY
REALLY BIG
BECAUSE YOU
CAN DO REALLY
BIG, AMAZING
THINGS!

WORK HARD,
BE KIND, AND
ALWAYS SAY
THANK YOU!

1
2
1
3

YOU ARE
AMAZING!
KEEP
SMILING!

GIVE
YOURSELF
A BIG HUG,
YOU'RE DOING
GREAT!

IT'S
GOING TO BE
A GREAT
GREAT DAY!

ALWAYS
LOOK FOR
A RAINBOW,
IT'S THERE TO
REMIND YOU
THAT YOU CAN DO
ANYTHING!

YOU ARE
SUPER SUPER
SMART!

SMILE
AT EVERYONE
TODAY!
IT WILL MAKE
YOUR HEART
HAPPY!

SPARKLE
ON!
SHINE
BRIGHT!

BE LIKE A
FLUFFY CLOUD!
HAPPY, CALM, AND
FLOAT TOWARDS
YOUR GOALS
AND DREAMS!

LOVE
EVERYTHING
ABOUT YOURSELF
BECAUSE
EVERYTHING
ABOUT YOU IS
AMAZING!

TRY
SOMETHING NEW
AND WATCH
HOW YOU GROW
AND GROW
AND GROW!

YOUR
SUPERPOWER
IS BELIEVING
IN YOURSELF!
YOU ARE
INCREDIBLE!
BELIEVE!

"YOU ARE
ROCKIN'
AT LIFE!
KEEP IT UP!"

YOU ARE
TOTALLY
THE BEST!

KEEP SMILING
AND GREAT
THINGS CAN
HAPPEN!

TRUST
YOUR HEART
AND
EVERYTHING
WILL BE OK!

YOU ARE
SO BEAUTIFUL AND
INCREDIBLE!
ALWAYS
REMEMBER THAT!

HELP SOMEONE
IN NEED AND
IT WILL BRIGHTEN
THEIR DAY
AND YOUR DAY
TOO!

YOU ARE
SOOOO
SPECIAL!

YOU
GOT
THIS!

DREAM

EXTRA BIG AND

EXTRA BIG

WONDERFUL THINGS

CAN HAPPEN

TO YOU!

BELIEVE
IN YOURSELF
AND YOU CAN
SOAR LIKE A
ROCKET SHIP
TO YOUR
DREAMS!

LOVE YOURSELF
BECAUSE
YOU ARE
SO AMAZING
AND
SO SPECIAL!

BE BRAVE,
BE STRONG!
YOU GOT
THIS!

BE A LEADER!
SHOW THE WORLD
WHAT
YOU CAN DO!

EVERYTHING
ABOUT YOU
IS AWESOME!

SHINE BRIGHT!
YOU ARE
A SUPERSTAR!

HEY SUNSHINE!
YOUR SMILE
IS AS BRIGHT AS
THE SUN!
KEEP SMILING!

YOU ARE
SO SO
LOVABLE!

TODAY
IS GOING TO BE
A GREAT,
GREAT DAY!

SMILE TODAY,
IT WILL MAKE
YOU FEEL
EXTRA HAPPY!

WHEN
YOU'RE HAVING
A BAD DAY,
SOMETIMES
YOU JUST NEED
A HUG!

TODAY IS
AN AWESOME DAY
AND YOU ARE
AWESOME TOO.
ENJOY IT!

YOU ARE
A SUPERSTAR!
KEEP ROCKING
AT LIFE!

LAUGH
EVERY DAY!
IT'S
THE BEST!

START
YOUR DAY WITH
A BIG BIG
HAPPY SMILE!

HEY,
YOU ARE
AMAZING!

DRAW
your own happy quote!

WRITE your own happy quote!

“

”

DRAW
your own happy quote!

WRITE
your own happy quote!

“

”

About the author

Kristen Griffin loves inspiring others and spreading positivity!
She is the author of the Happy series -Happy Clouds, Happy Words and Happy Quotes- bringing lots of smiles to readers!
She lives with her husband and two children, who inspire her every day.
Her goal is to spread a little more happiness in the world.

About the illustrator

Giorgia Isacchi is a graphic designer with the passion for children's illustrations.
She illustrated children books for various clients from all over the world.
She loves to create unique and engaging artworks from her home studio that she shares with her family and her beloved dog.
Through her illustrations she aims to make people smile and dream.

PLEASE VISIT US ONLINE AT

www.happyhappyeverything.com

www.ingramcontent.com/pod-product-compliance
Lightning Source LLC
LaVergne TN
LVHW070136110826
845147LV00002B/263

9798995972006